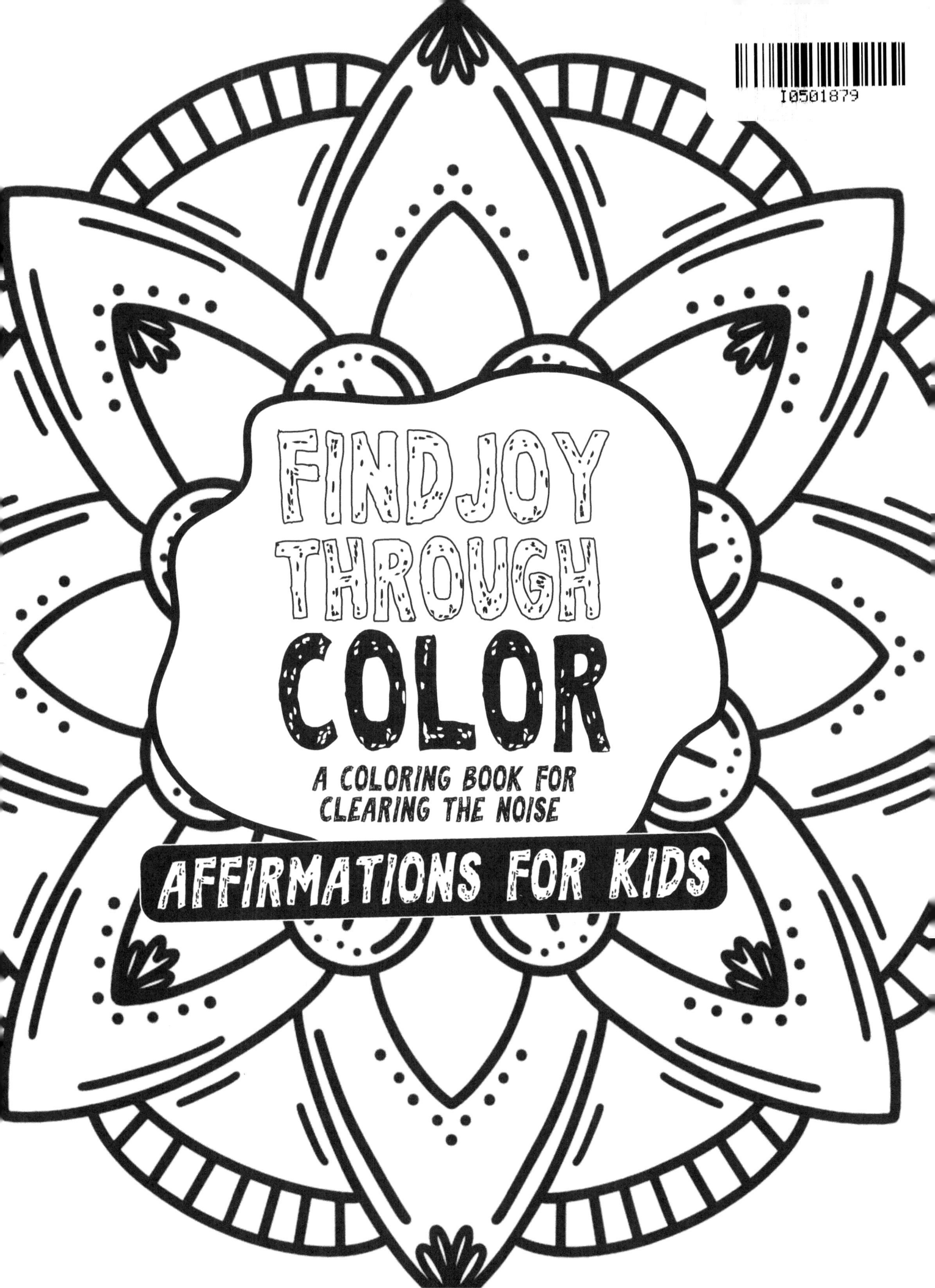

# HEY, KID! IT'S TIME TO GET YOUR COLOR ON

So often we find ourselves filling our minds with words that hold too much weight. Think about the last thing you said to yourself today. Was it positive and filled with love?

Next time you have a bad day or a tough moment, remember to be kind to yourself and speak words of love and light. Challenge yourself to fill your heart and soul with affirmations that will uplift your spirit and hold fast to your mind.

May the coloring pages in this book begin your journey to clearing the noise and speaking life over yourself daily!

## SPECIAL NOTE

You will notice on the back of each illustration is a blacked out page.

For those that love markers and gel pens and any other heavy mediums, this black page is to help avoid color bleeding through to the next page.

While color pencils and crayons are the recommended tool for this book, I know that sometimes markers can cover more canvas. Think of this as some extra insurance so you can fill the pages as you please.

Thanks!

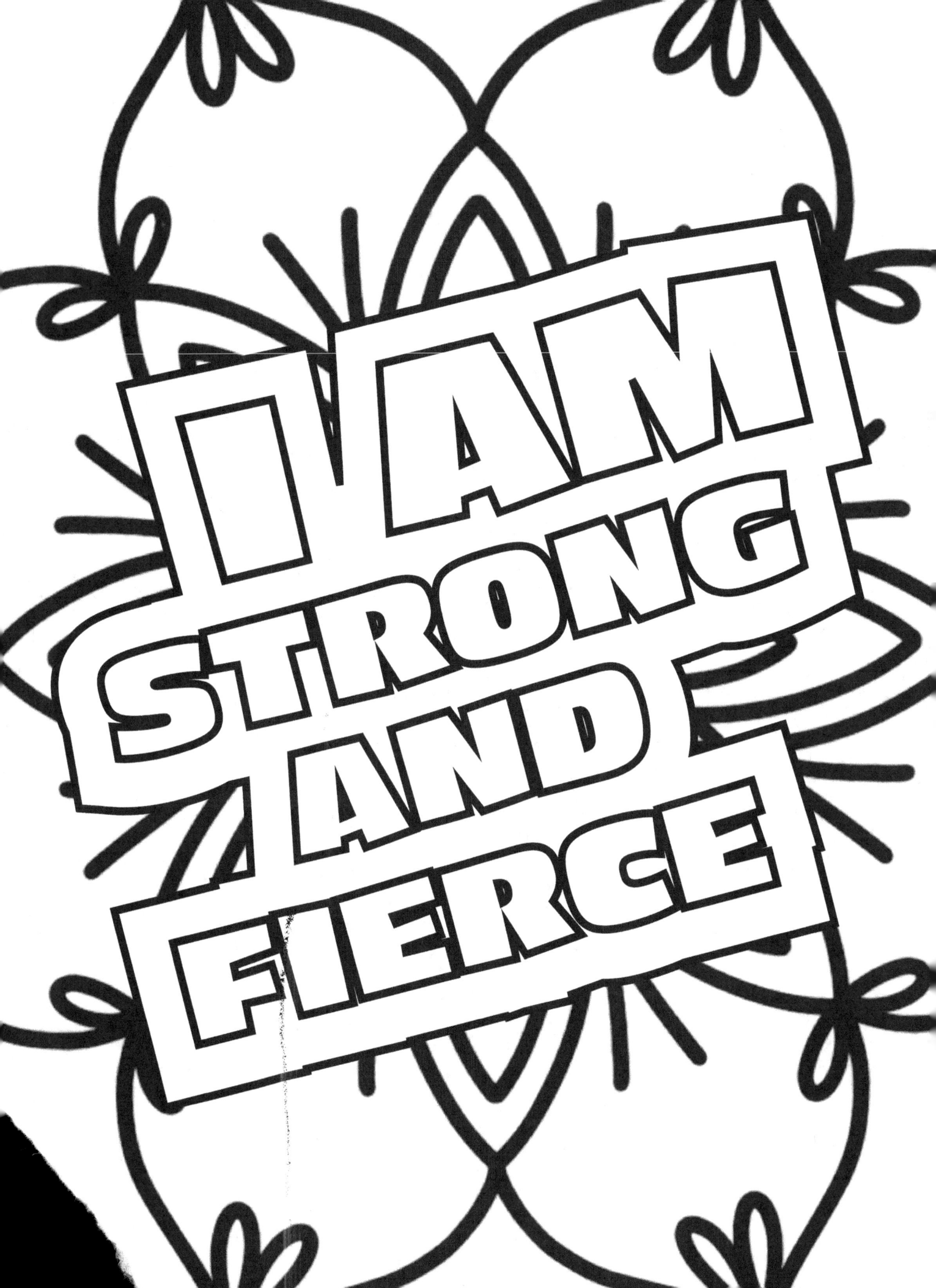

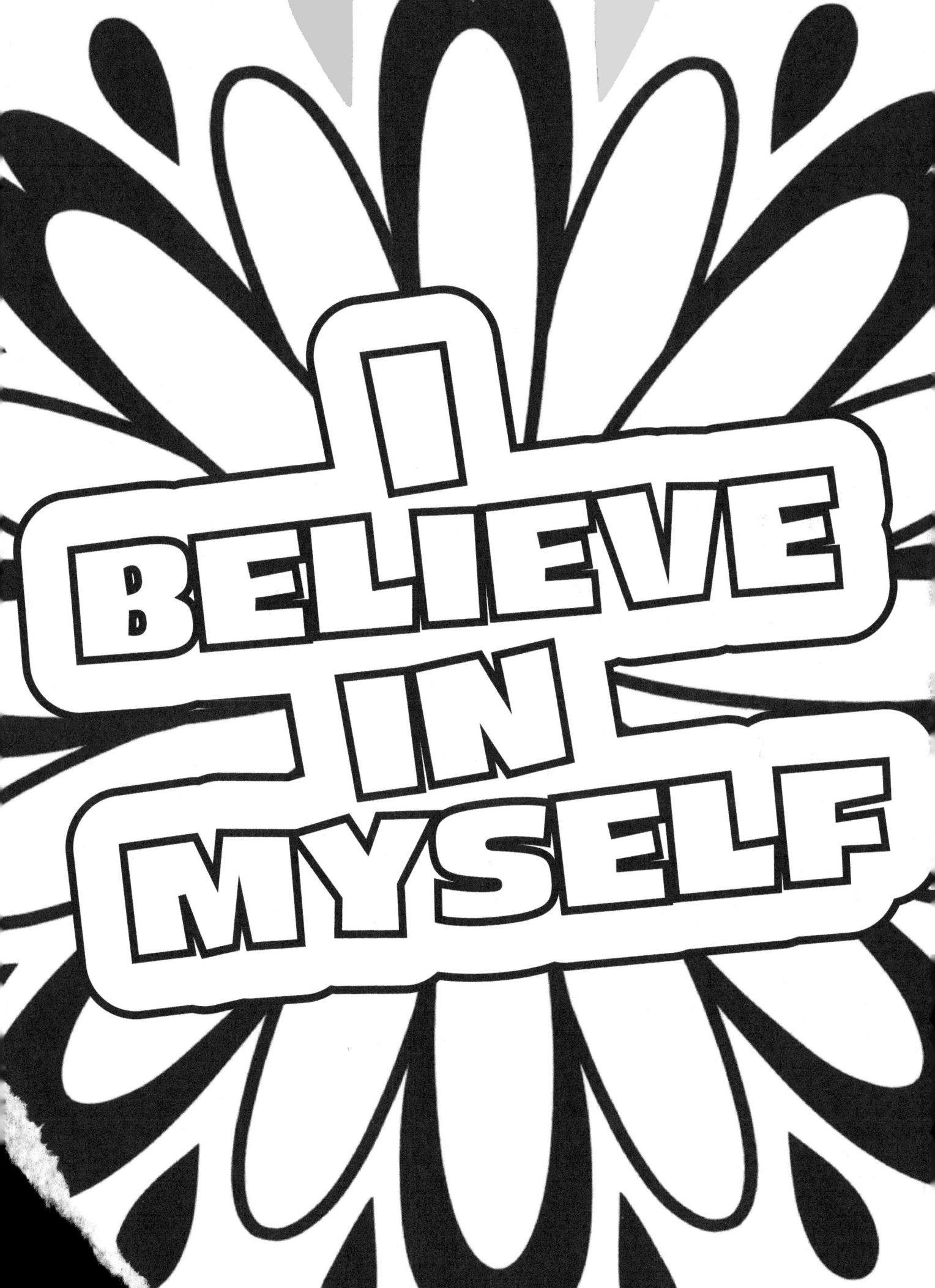

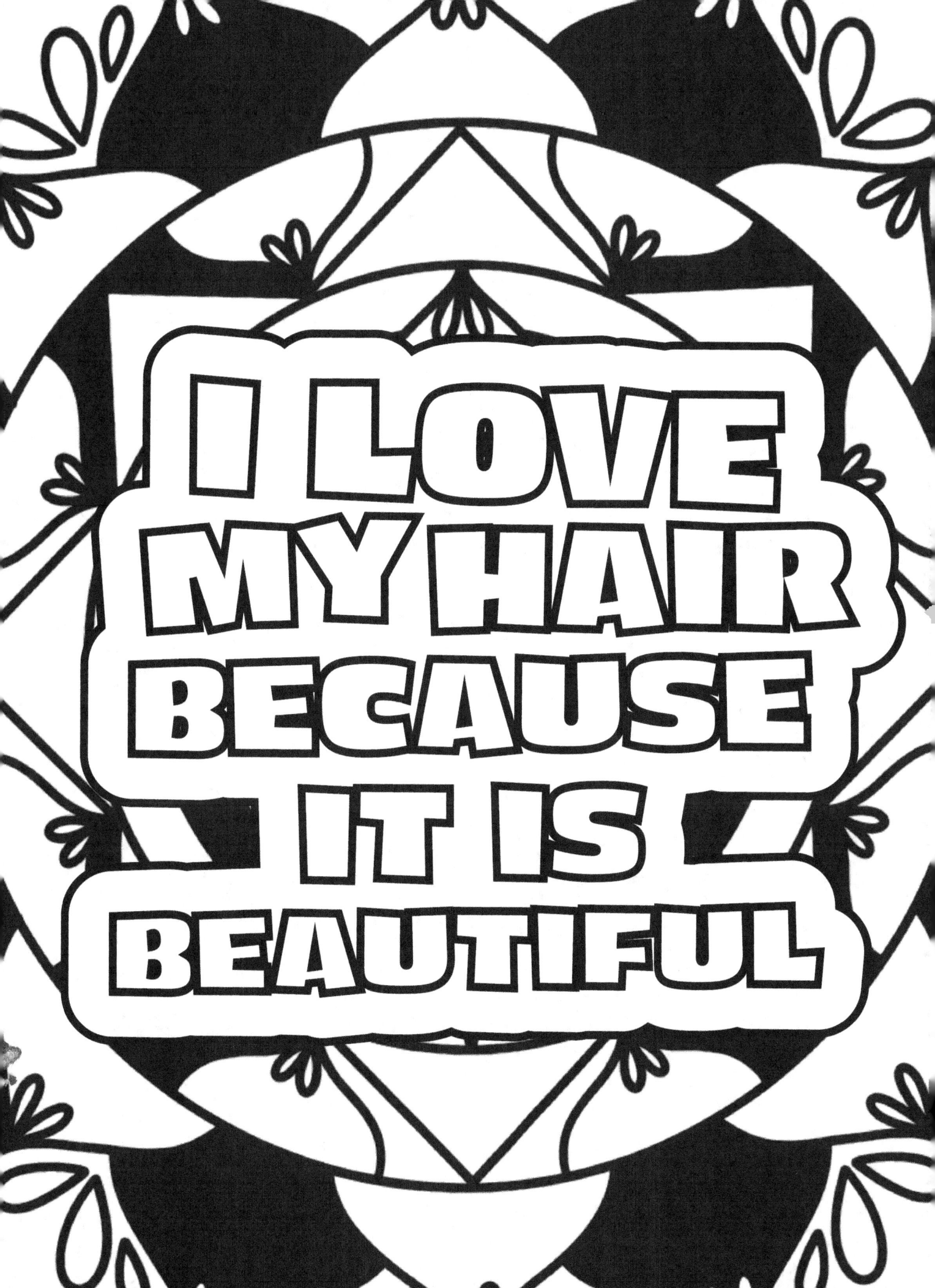

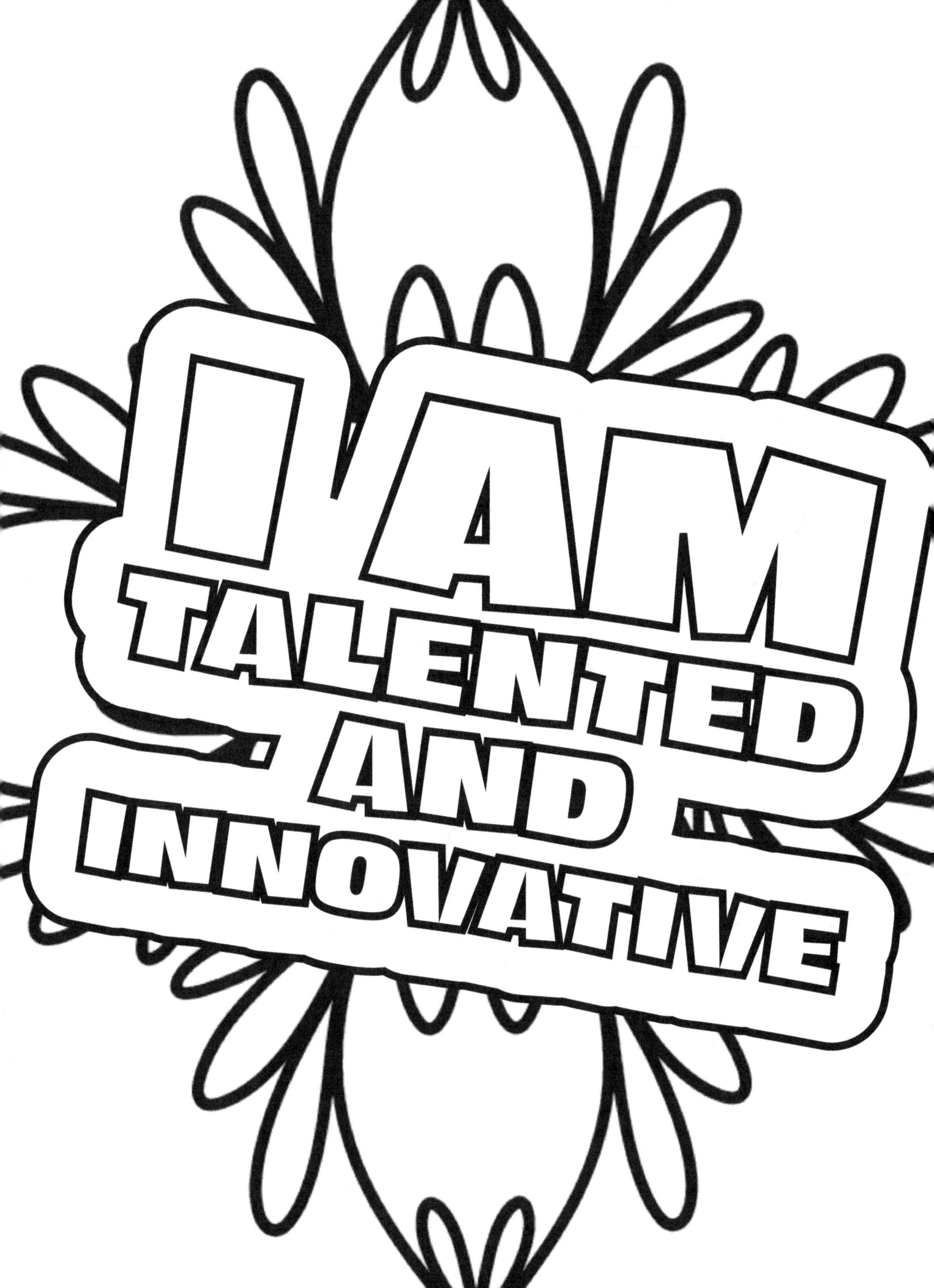

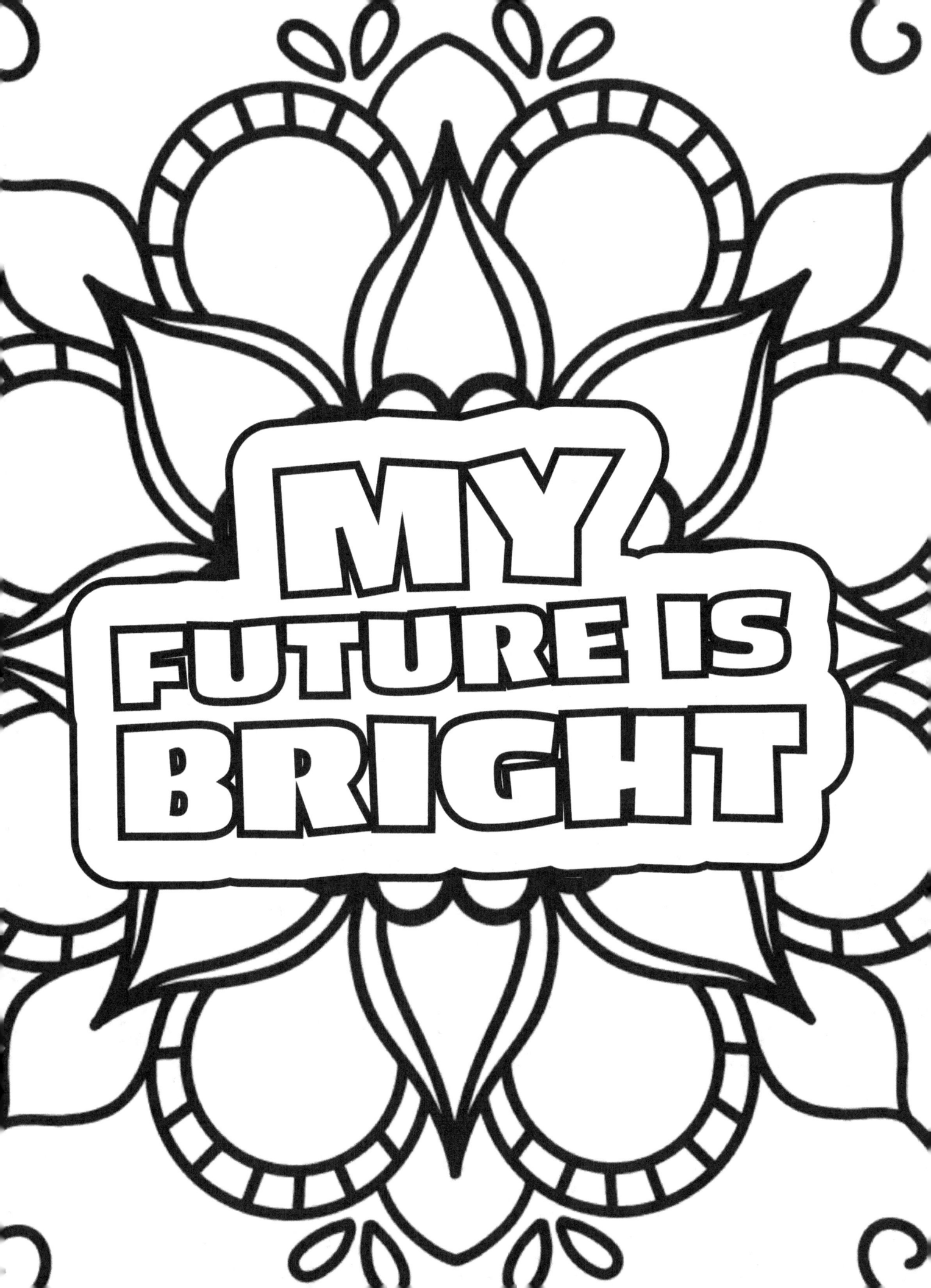

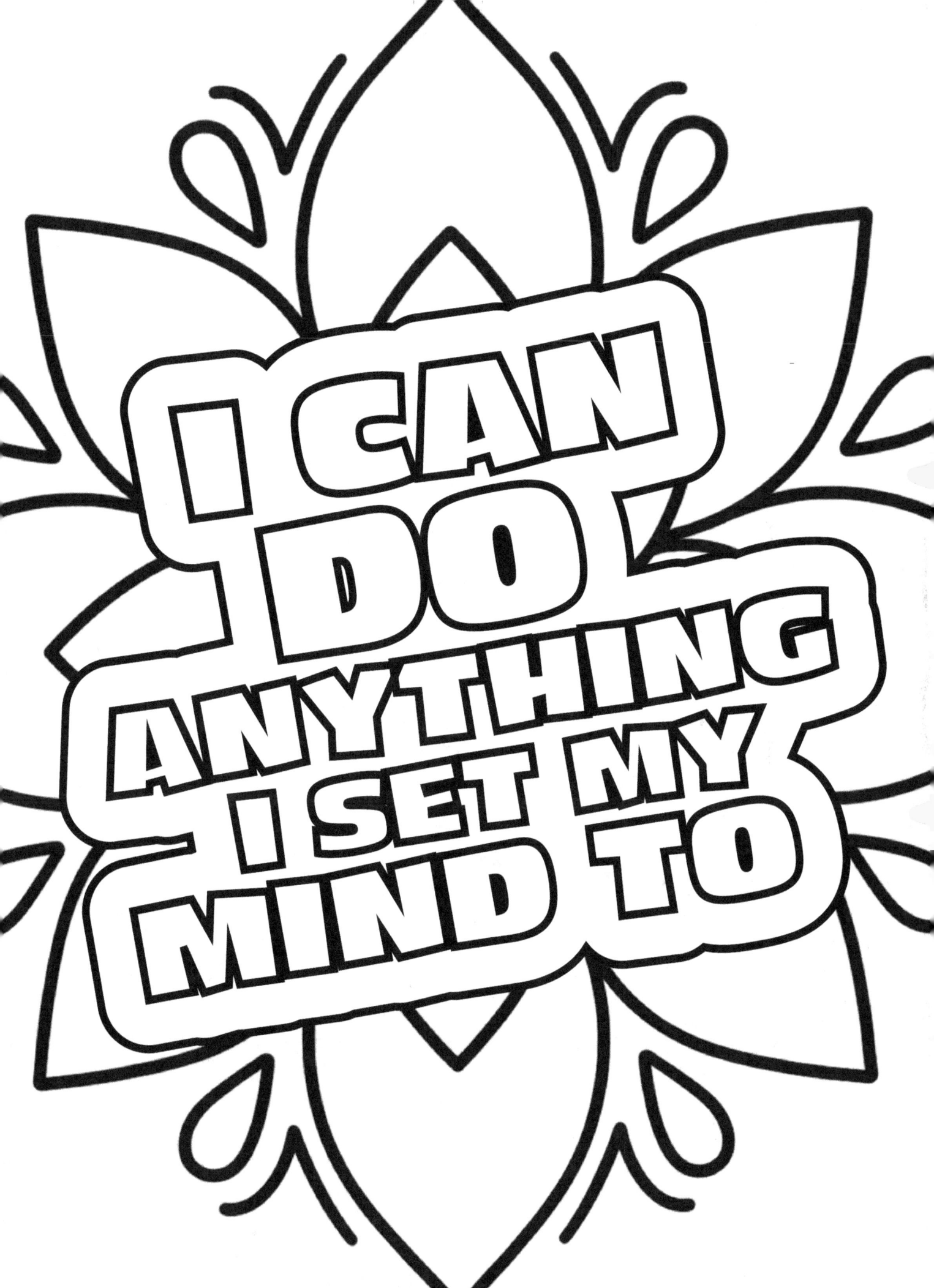

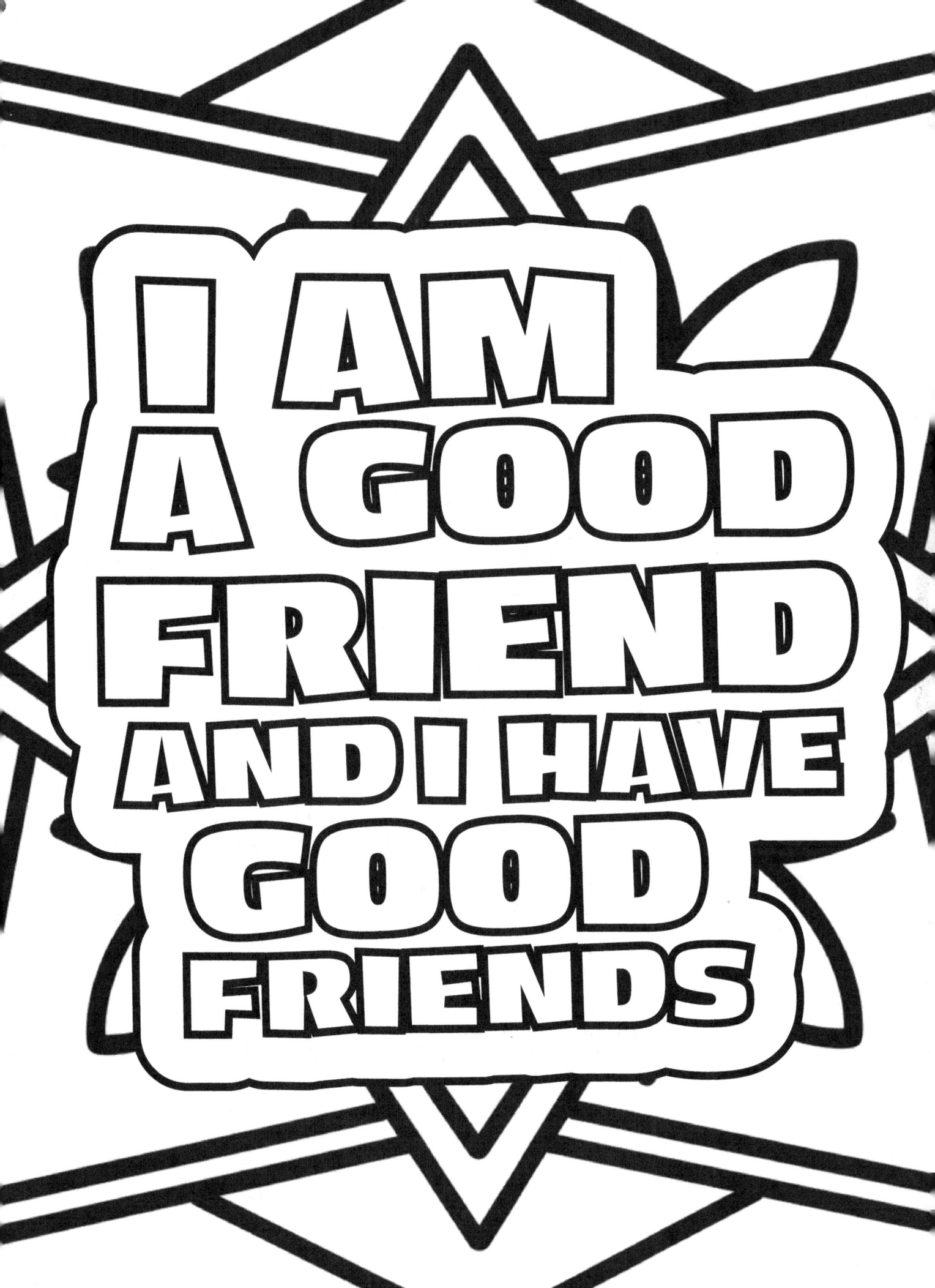

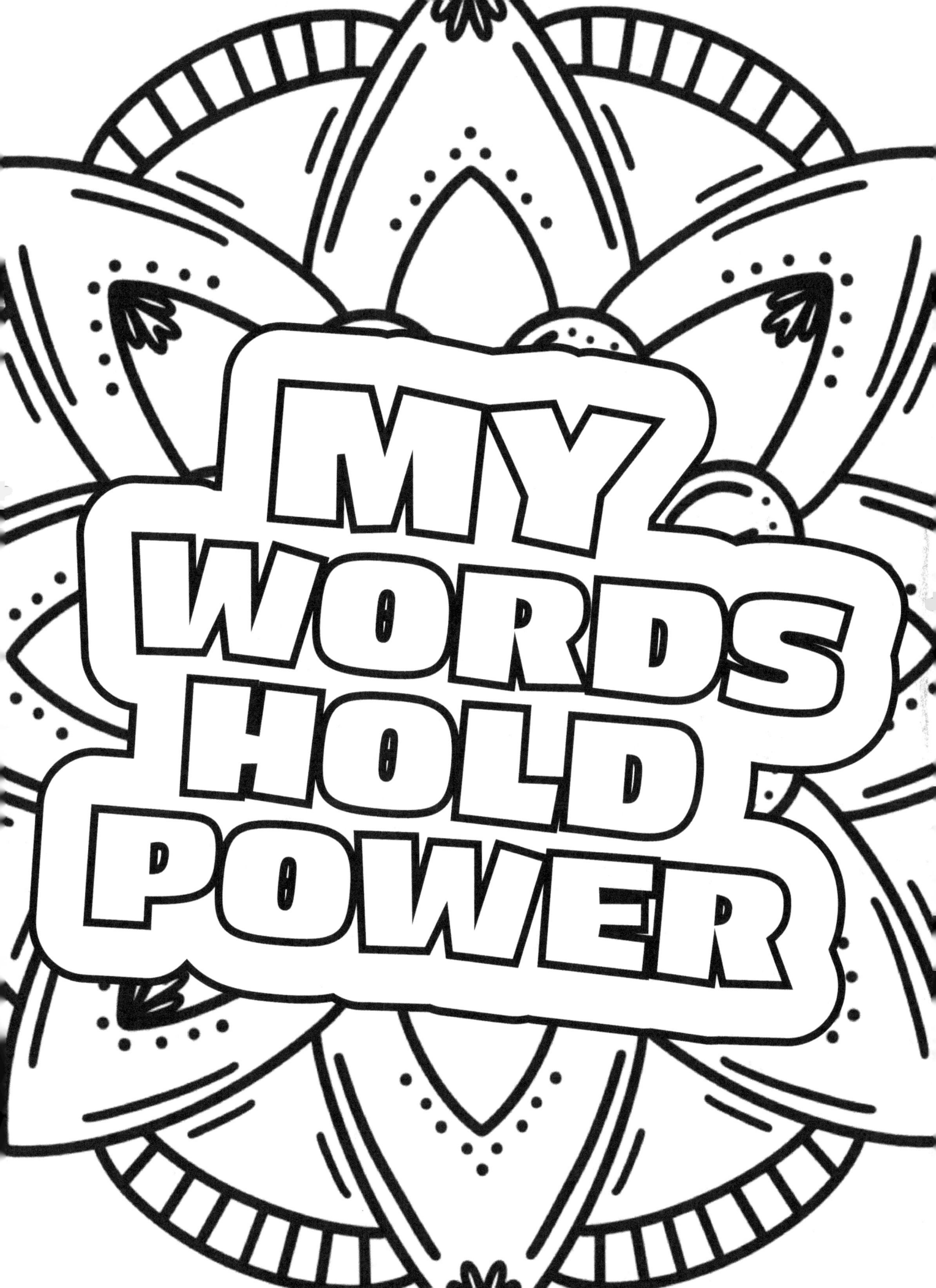

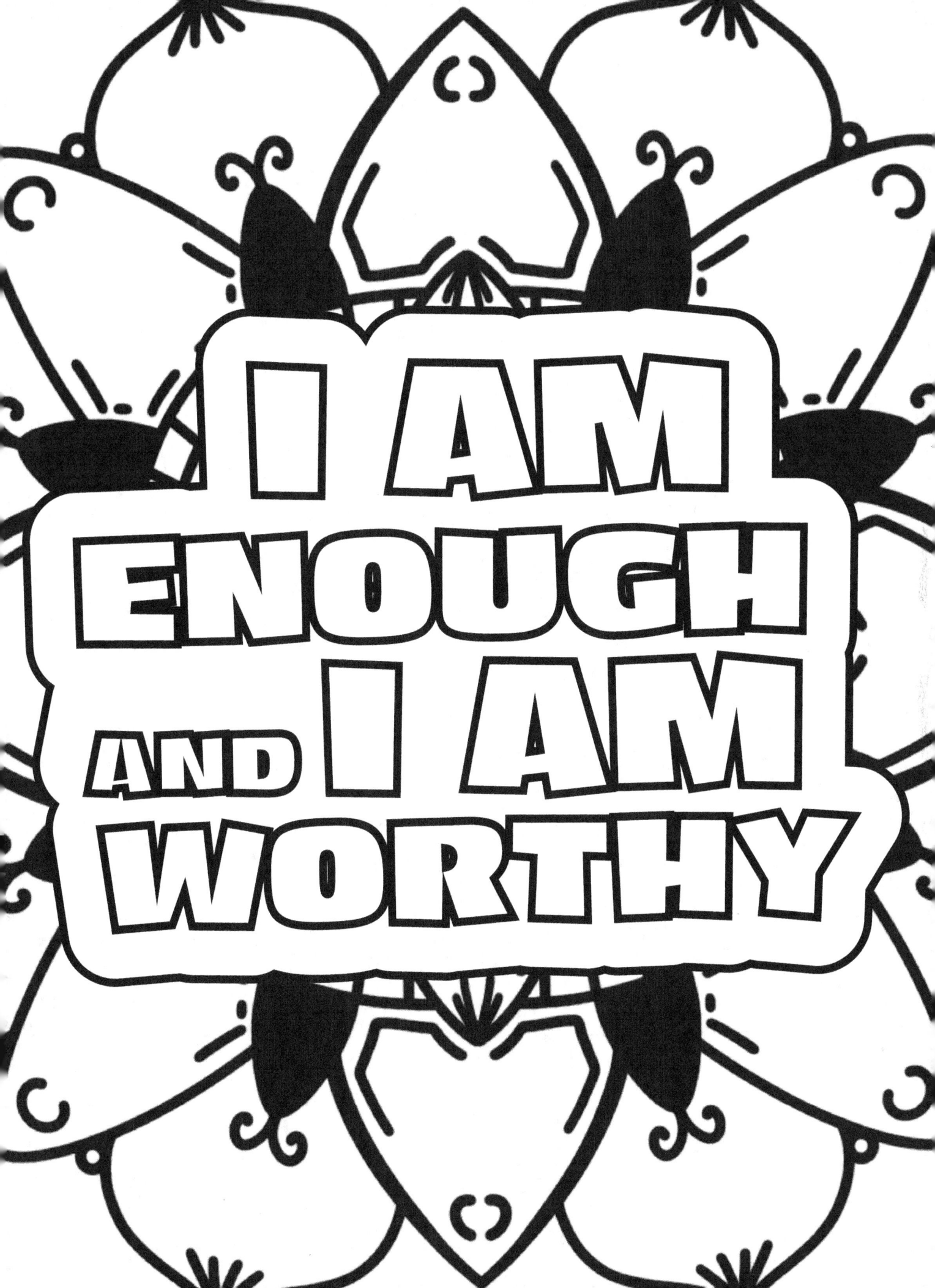

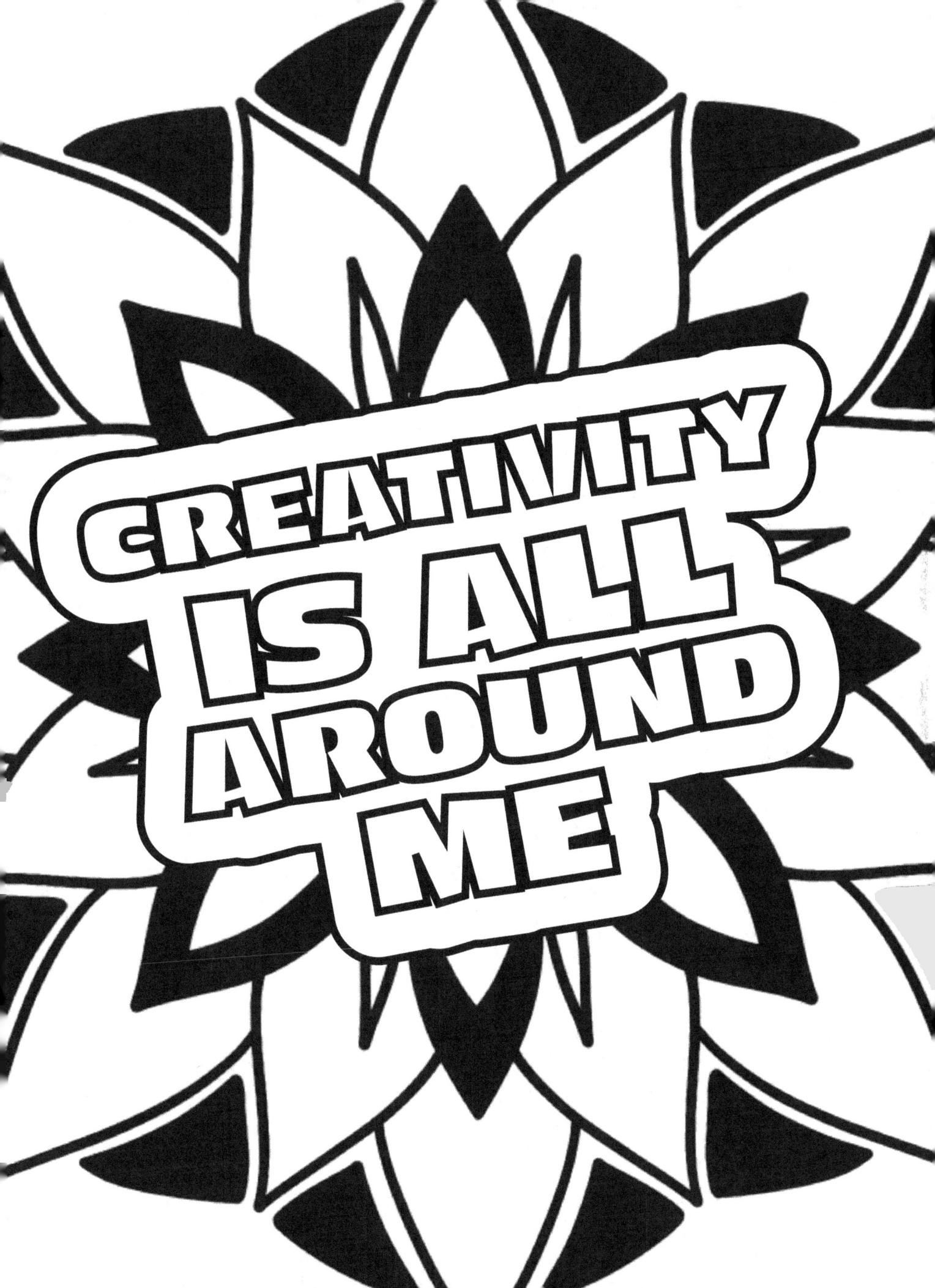

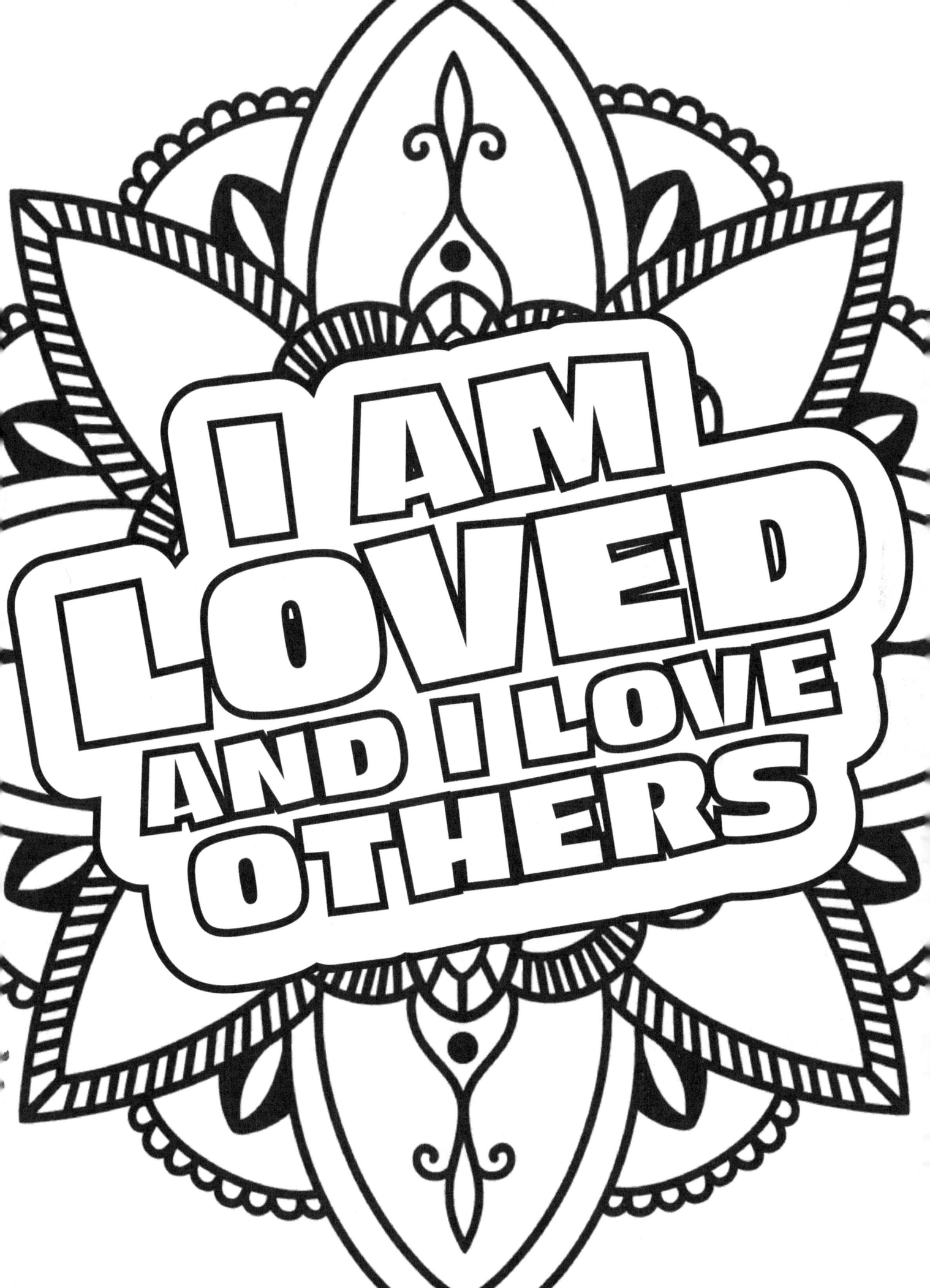

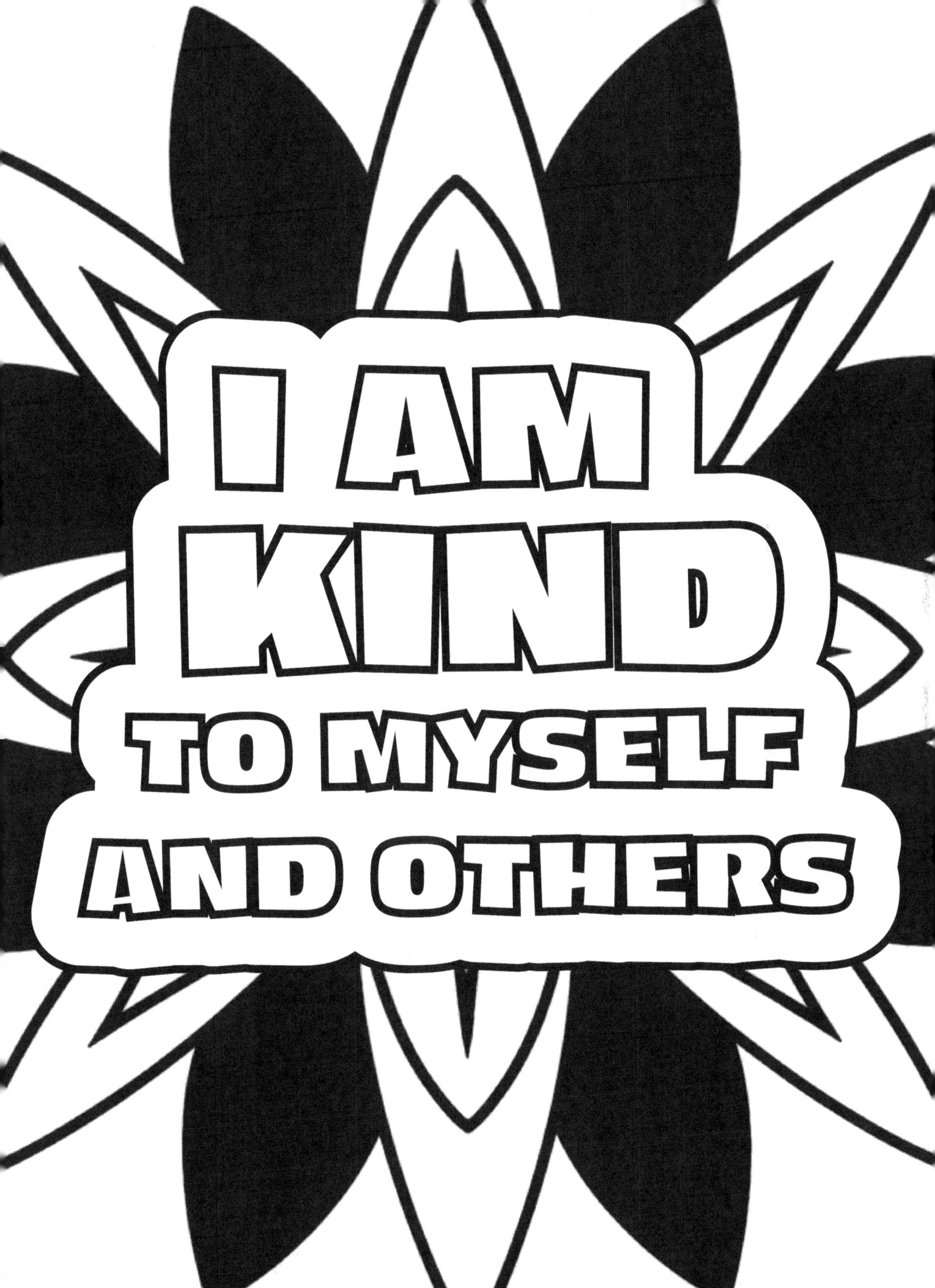

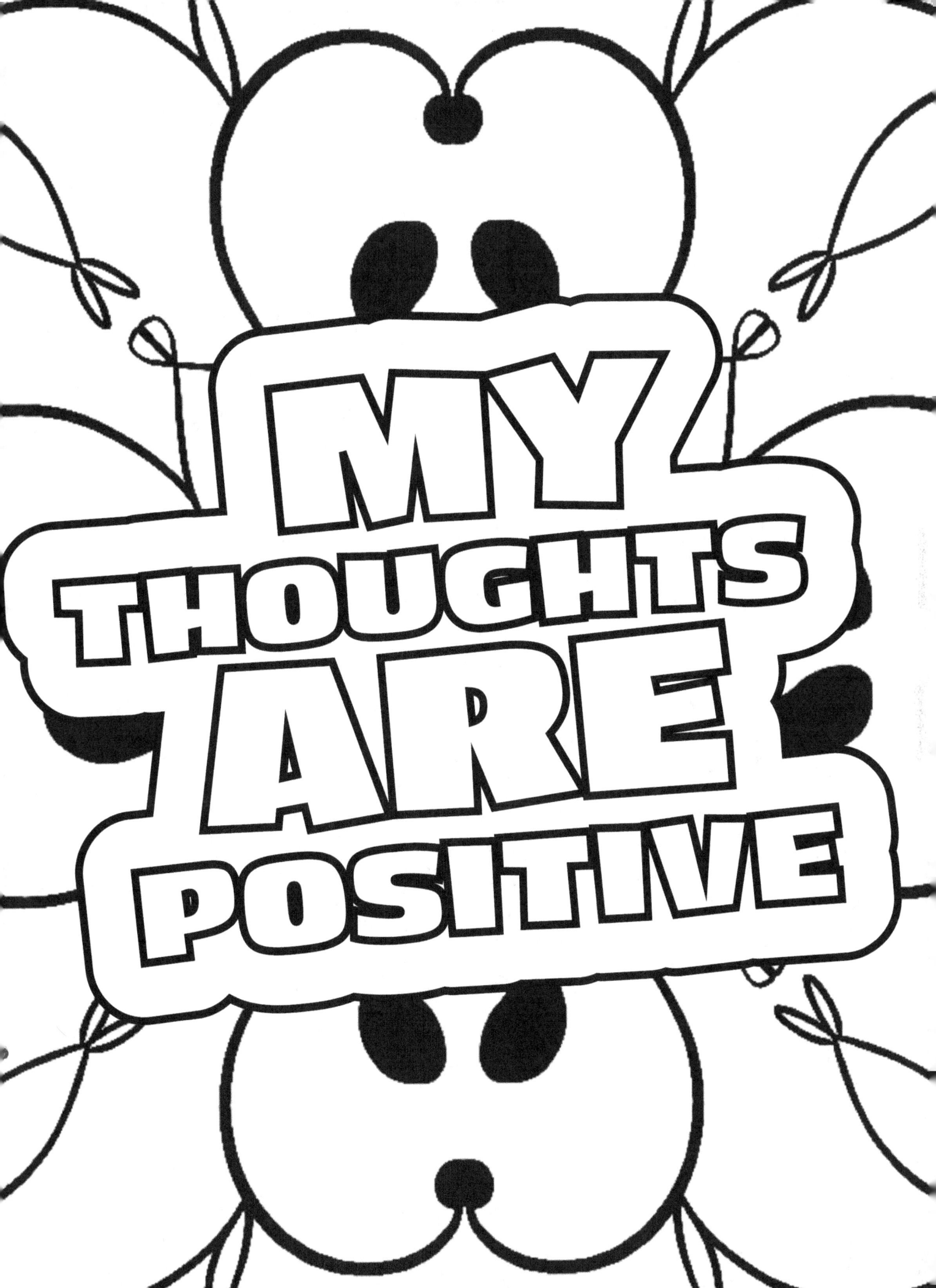

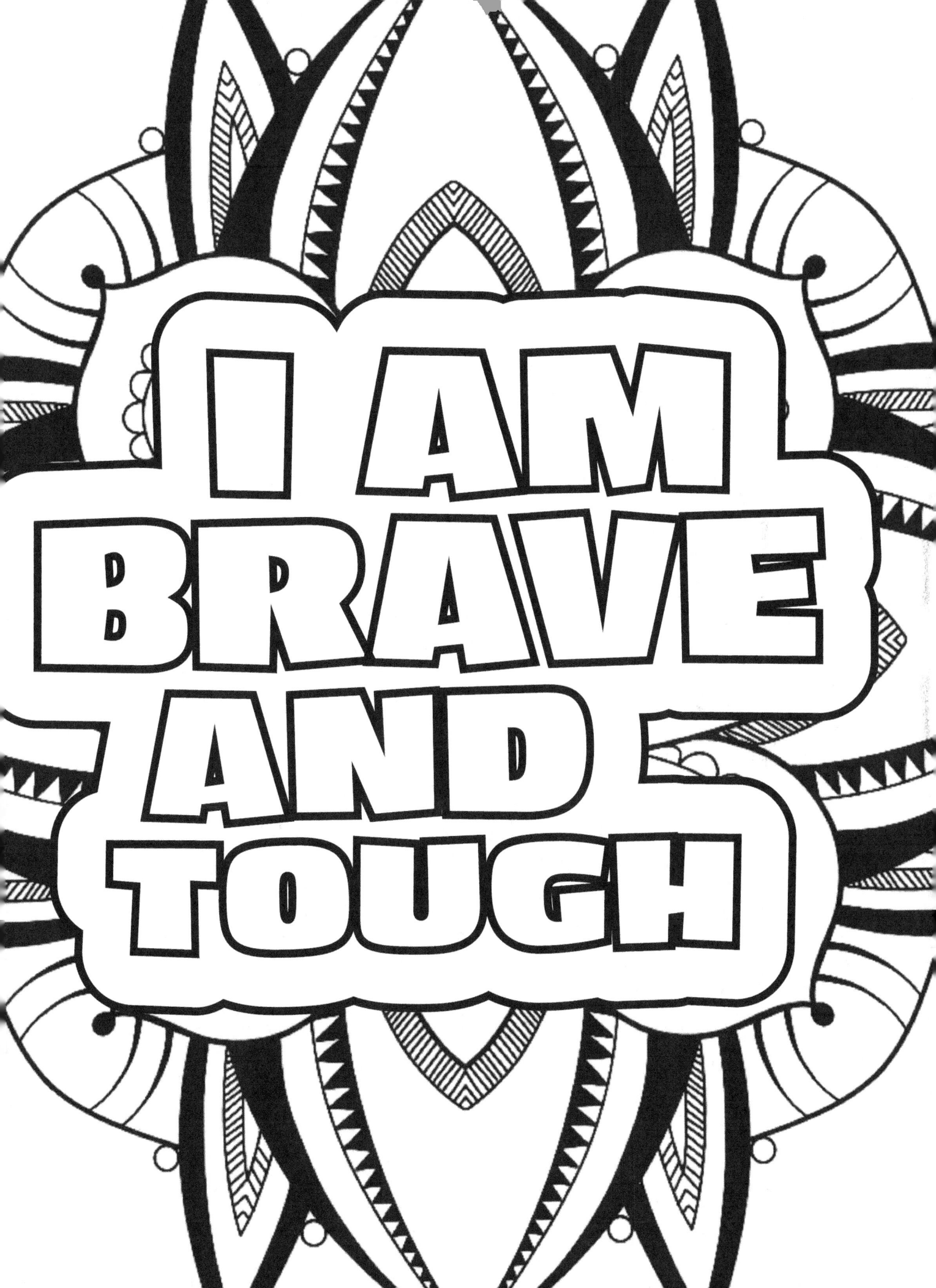

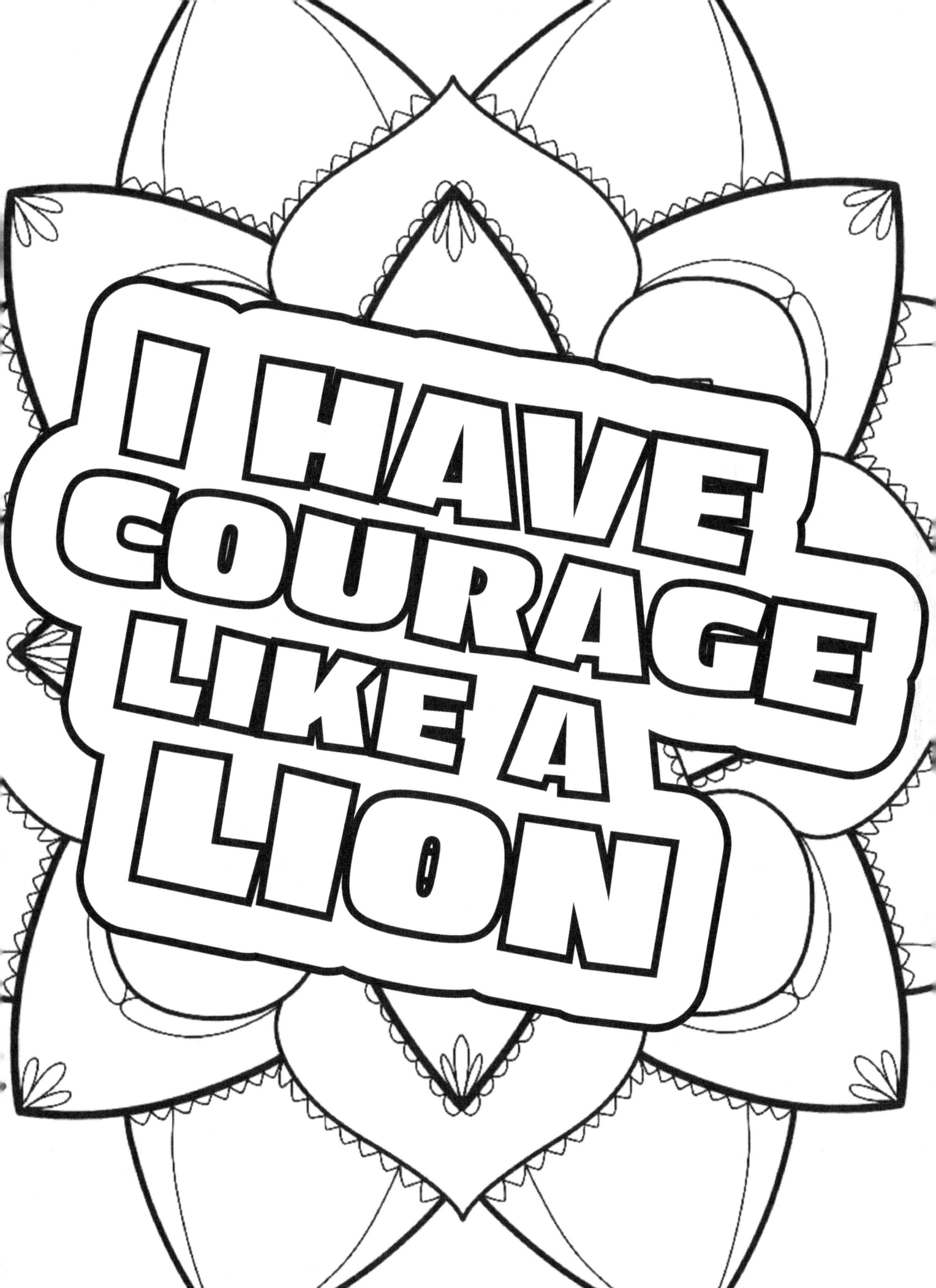

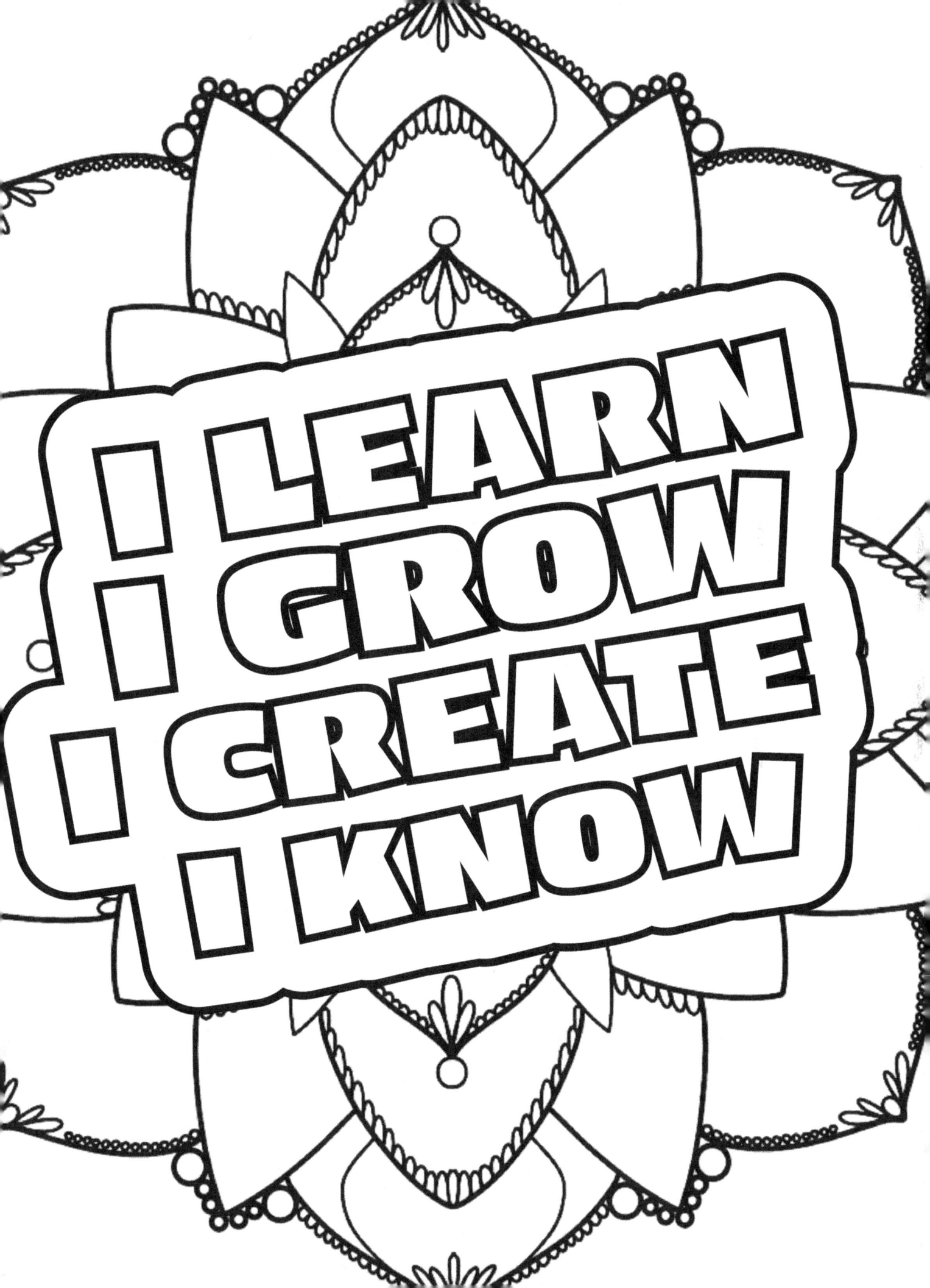

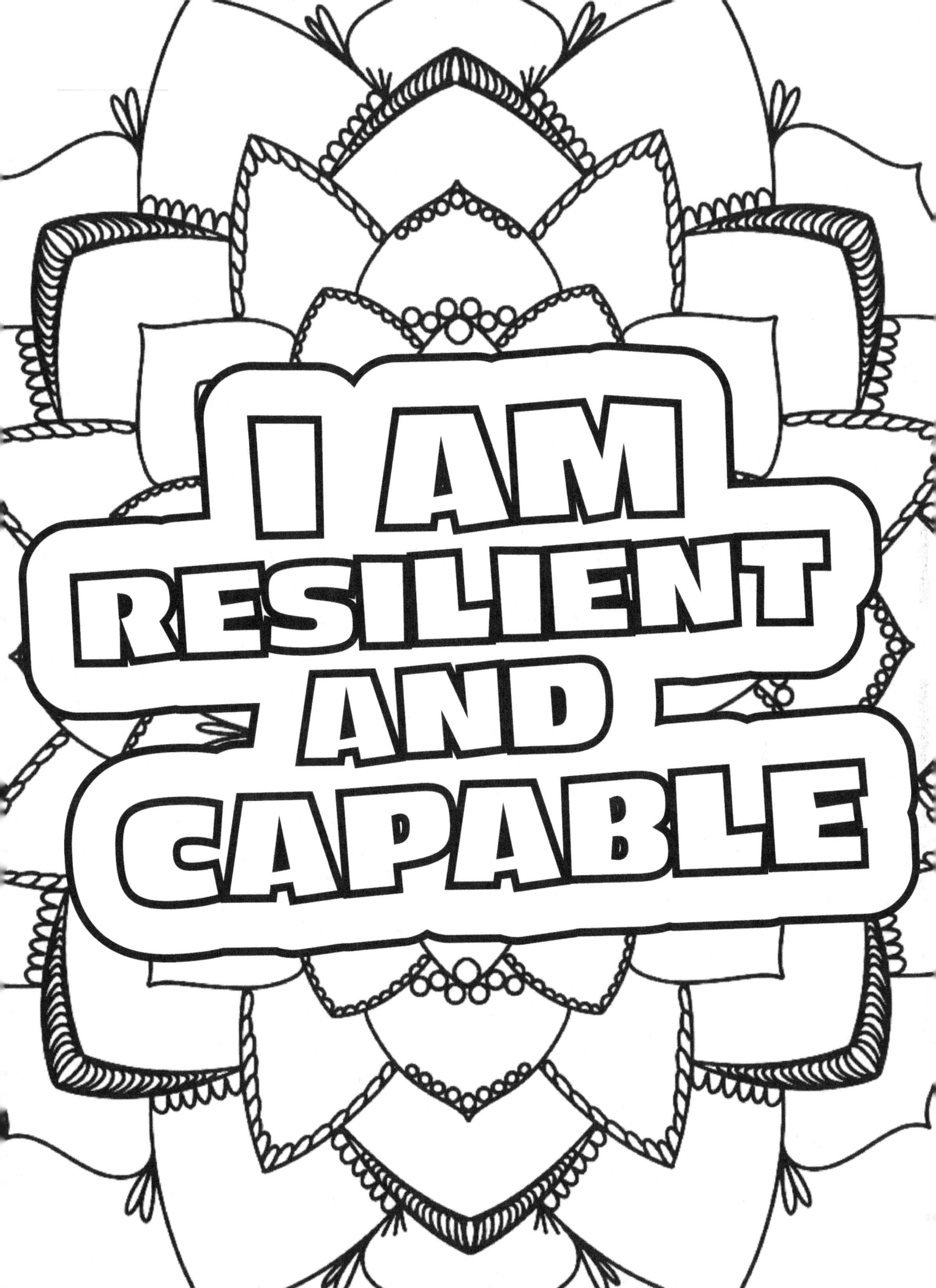

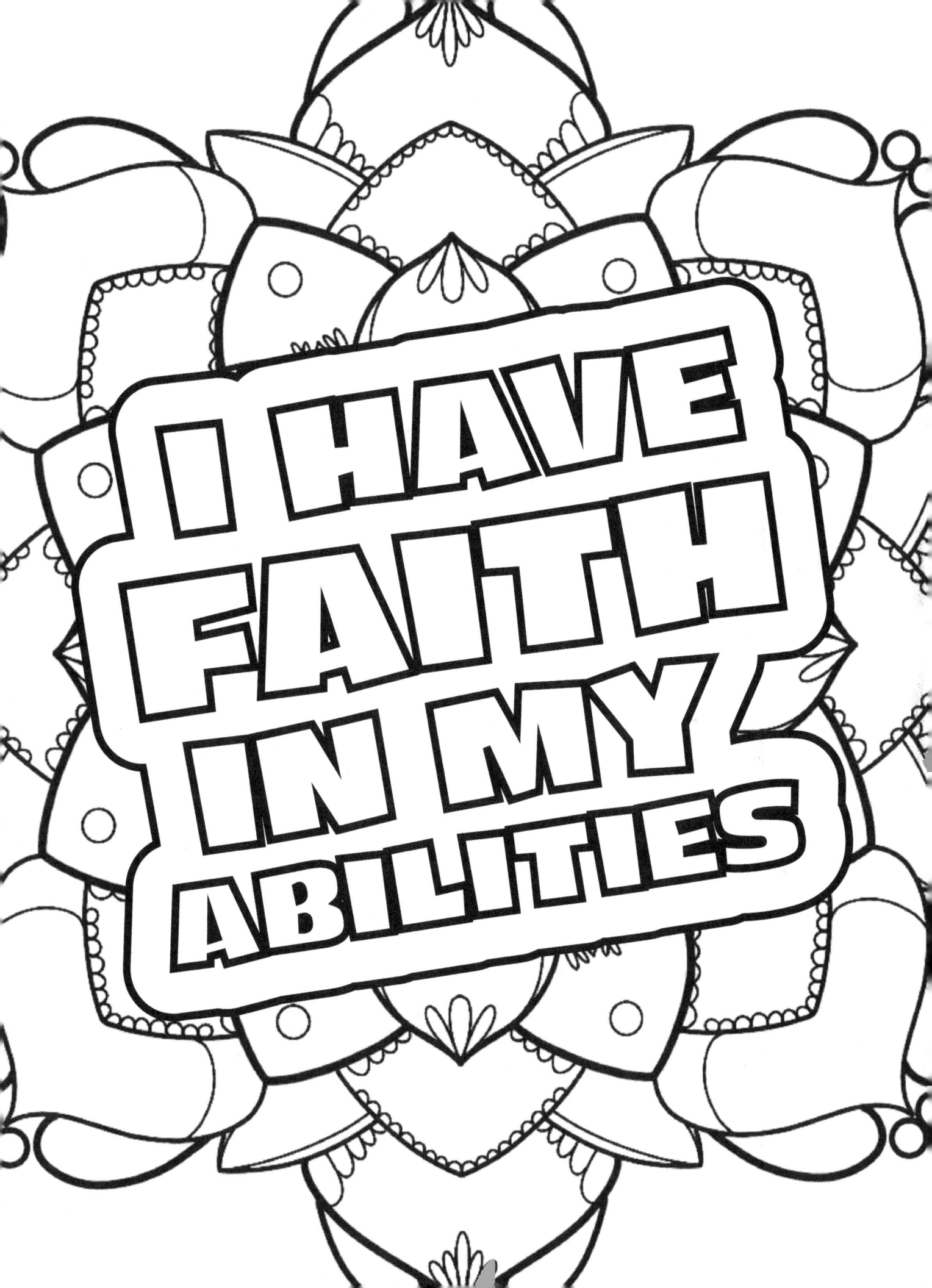

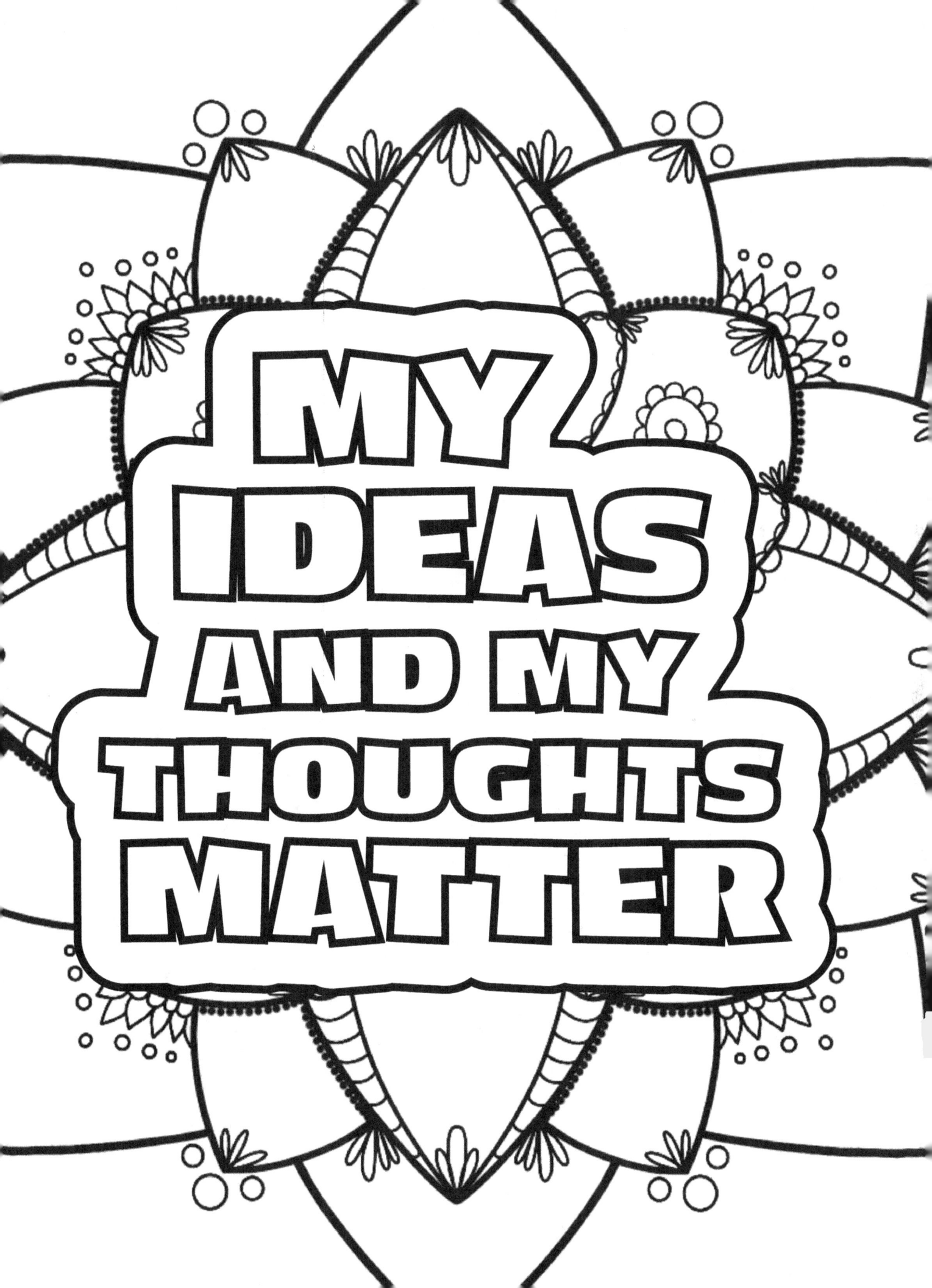

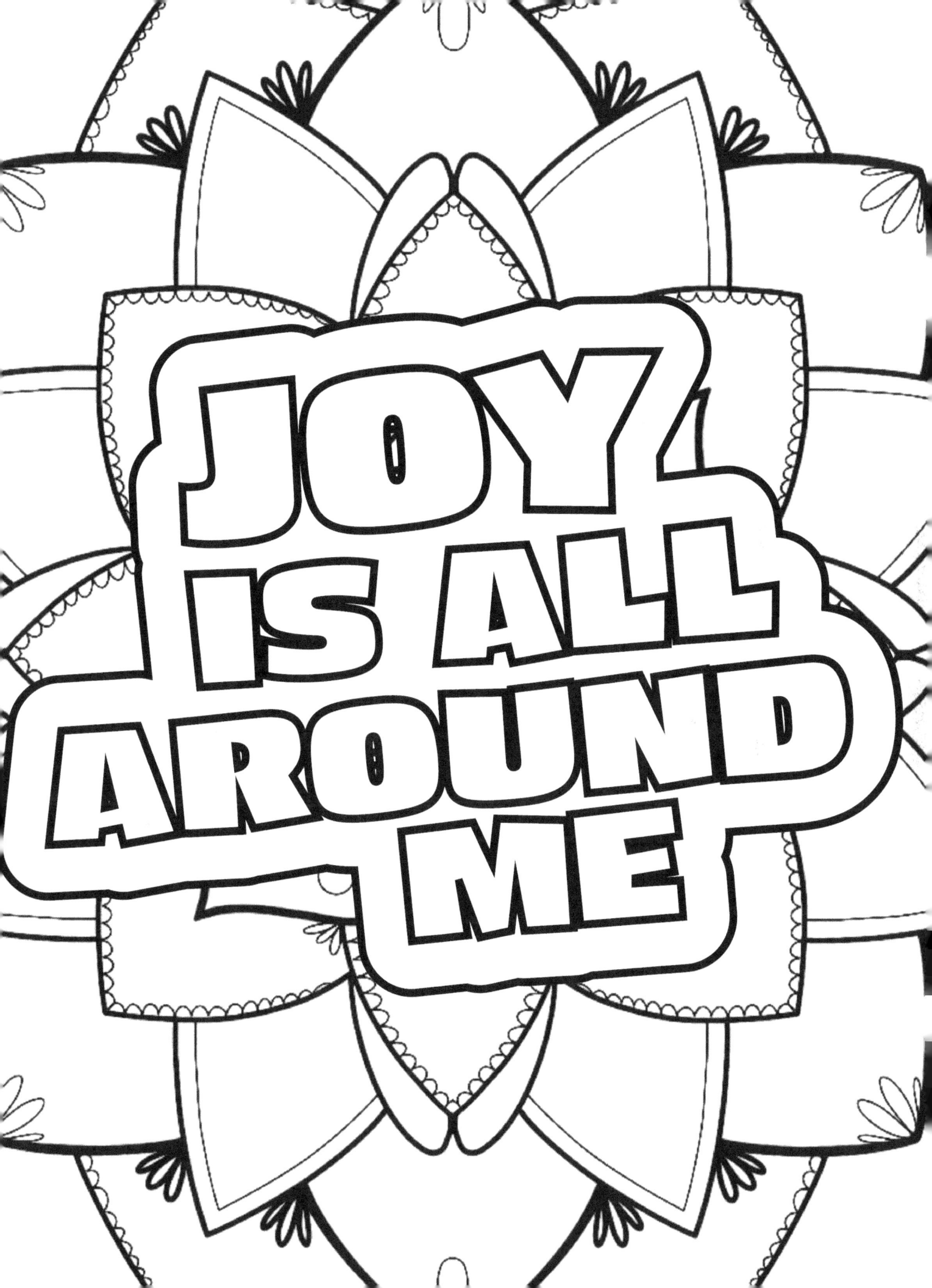

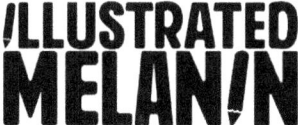

Designed in Joy. Created with Love.

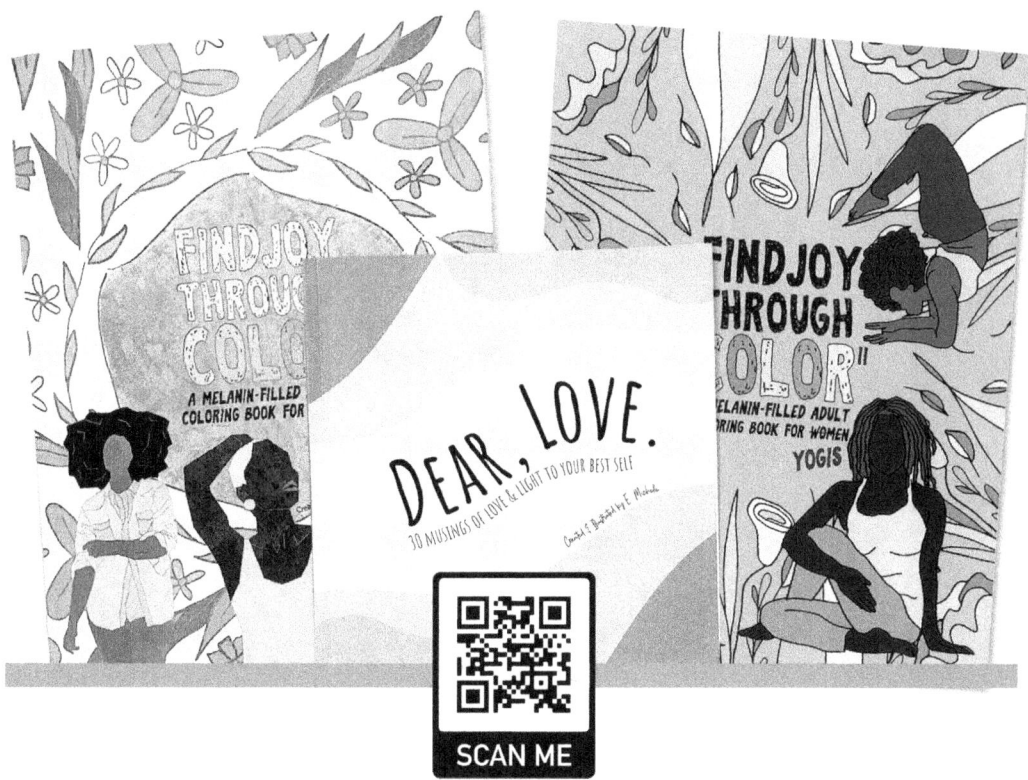

Subscribe to illustratedmelanin.com for more inspiration.

Written & Illustrated by E Michelle

© 2024 by Illustrated Melanin. All rights reserved. No part of this publication may be reproduced or transmitted in any form or by any means, electronic or mechanical, including photocopy or recording. All copyright remains with Illustrated Melanin and is non-transferable. Contact the author via email: hello@illustratedmelanin.com with any questions.

www.ingramcontent.com/pod-product-compliance
Lightning Source LLC
Chambersburg PA
CBHW062126220526
45471CB00010B/3898